Mila's Meditation

Céline Combet

To order additional copies of this book, contact:
Xlibris
844-714-8691
www.Xlibris.com
Orders@Xlibris.com

ISBN: Softcover   978-1-6641-9361-1
       Hardcover   978-1-6641-9362-8
       EBook   978-1-6641-9360-4

Print information available on the last page

Rev. date: 09/08/2021

To my little Buddha, I am grateful that you chose me as your mother. Simply by you being present in my life taught me so much. I love you to the moon and stars.

I am a young Girl full of Energy,
And quite busy, I am going to School
to my Physical Activities,
to see my Family, my Friends.

My Life is a Flower,
The Earth in which I am growing
Is my Activity,
The Love of the people who love me
Of my Family, my friends,
Is what nurtures my Energy.

So like all beautiful flowers,
I Spray myself...

Not with Water, of course !
Meditation is a special Moment for Me,
Which I like to practice in the Car,
Between each Activity,
When I am coming in the class,
Before eating dinner or lunch, before sleeping.
It helps me to see better, feel better,
understand better,
To hear, to Speak,
And to focus.
It helps me to feel comfortable
And to feel good in everything I do.

Do you want to learn
with me ?

Great !
So, first off, you inhale deeply.
It means that I swallow some air,
And I inflate my belly until it becomes very big.
It is funny, but I stay focus
In my breathing.
Then, I exhale, it means
I reject the air very deeply
with a heart-shaped mouth.
I do it three times to let my body
know that the meditation starts.

I inhale...
I exhale...

My body is the stem of my Flower,
So for the Lifeblood to flow
I guide it and I teach it how to empty itself.
To do that, I am contracting my Body hard,
Very hard, my whole Body,
And my face...
And I am inhaling at the same time
Harder, again... and I let go... and I exhale.
I am doing this over three times.
At this moment I am closing my Eyes.

Mila contracts her whole Body.

And this is where my moment starts,
This is when I am watering my flower.
With my eyes closed, I am nurishing myself
With this special moment just for me.
I am picturing myself in a Bubble
Of the color of my choice.
I inhale...
I exhale,
I am picturing some beautiful roots
Under my feet, to seek
All the love of the Earth's Heart energy.
I exhale,
Cette belle énergie verte émeraude brillante
Et cristalline remonte dans mon corps,
Mon cœur et dans ma bulle.

And I exhale gently...

I inhale...

My Bubble is now made of a Shiny Green,
And Shiny of a Golden Dust,
And diamonds.

This Light is inside of me,
Around me,
It kisses me,
And hugs me.

I feel good,
And nourished by the Energy
Of the Earth and the Sun.

I exhale,
I am spoiled with this
Very special Gift,
For the Flower that I am.

I inhale this Light to enjoy it better,
And for it to nurture me,
My whole Body,
My arms, my legs,
My heart, etc.

I am inhaling this Light full of Love,
In my Crystal Clear Bubble,
And some Golden Dust flows in my Bubble,
My Body and My Heart.

I exhale......

I breathe calmly
And gently.
I am in my Bubble,
Relaxed, secured, quiet,
Focus, with a Kind Attitude.
And I open my Eyes whenever I feel like it,
To end my Meditation.
I am like a Flower who creates Joy
Around me.
I am practicing all my sweet qualities
In each of my activities,
At School, with my family,
Or with my friends.

Can you tell me which are the qualities
You like to practice ?

For me, it is Gratitude.

The Sun and The Earth are also
Very proud of Me,
For I redistribute all the Love
They gave me.

I also think to thank them,
For it is important to show
That I appreciate the other's gesture.
This is why each night, I thank them,
For this day which arrives to its end,
For the Light that the Sun created,
And for having the Chance to live
On this beautiful Earth.

I am thanking them every morning,
For the new Day they give me
Which I am going to enjoy a lot.

Printed in the United States
by Baker & Taylor Publisher Services